WEATHER WATCH

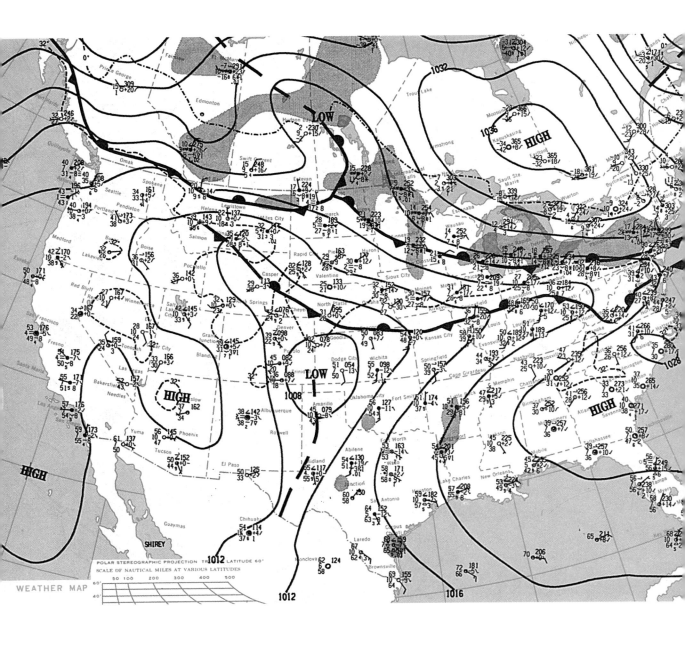

WEATHER MAP

WEATHER WATCH
FORECASTING THE WEATHER

by Jonathan D. W. Kahl

Lerner Publications Company / Minneapolis

For Samantha Rose

Front cover: Ken Barlow, chief meteorologist at KARE-TV, Minneapolis, Minnesota
Page 2: A special weather map for scientists, issued by the National Weather Service

Words printed in **bold** are explained in the glossary that begins on page 68.

Library of Congress Cataloging-in-Publication data

Kahl, Jonathan D.
    Weather watch : forecasting the weather / by Jonathan D. W. Kahl.
      p. cm. — (How's the weather?)
    Includes index.
    ISBN 0-8225-2529-1
      1. Weather — Juvenile literature. 2. Weather forecasting — Juvenile literature. 3. Weather — Experiments — Juvenile literature. [1. Weather. 2. Weather forecasting.] I. Title. II. Series.
    Kahl, Jonathan D. How's the weather?
    QC981.3.K33 1996
    551.6'3 — dc20   95-9725

Manufactured in the United States of America
1 2 3 4 5 6 – JR – 01 00 99 98 97 96

CONTENTS

INTRODUCTION

Of all the changes we experience in our lives, few are more constant or dramatic than changes in the weather. The day-to-day variation in weather has been around for billions of years, long before people or even animals lived on Earth.

Weather has always had a strong effect on people. In the earliest societies, hunting, fishing, and farming—the activities people needed for survival—were influenced by the weather. Weather still controls many aspects of our lives. A sudden snowstorm might force schools to close for the day. Dense fog might delay airplane flights and strand passengers at the airport. Some weather events can have tragic effects, such as floods following heavy rains or the destruction of homes by a tornado.

Since ancient times, people have wanted to understand the weather and have tried to predict when and how the weather would change. The ancient Greek philosopher Aristotle wrote a book about rain, snow, and other "meteors" that fall from the sky. Written in the fourth century B.C., Aristotle's *Meteorologica* gave a name to the modern science that deals with the

People who like to spend time outdoors often pay attention to weather forecasts.

weather—**meteorology**. Scientists who study and predict the weather are called meteorologists.

George Washington and other early American leaders kept daily weather records for many years. Thomas Jefferson, an avid weather-watcher, recorded a temperature of 76°F (Fahrenheit) on the afternoon of July 4, 1776, the day the Continental Congress adopted the Declaration of Independence. Benjamin Franklin, the most famous early American meteorologist, wrote *Poor Richard's Almanac*, a yearly publication containing weather **forecasts**, or predictions. Franklin's almanac is still issued today, under the name *Old Farmer's Almanac*.

In the early 1800s, meteorologists recorded the weather using only their eyes and a few simple instruments. They had no way to measure weather conditions many miles above the ground, nor could they easily communicate with other meteorologists to find out what the weather was like in surrounding areas. The invention in the 1840s of the telegraph, a device for sending electrical messages through wires, greatly improved the practice of weather forecasting. The telegraph allowed meteorologists to communicate with one another and to compare local conditions with weather far away. For the first time, scientists could track storms and other weather events as they moved across the country.

In 1870 President Ulysses S. Grant assigned to the U.S. military, which operated a nationwide telegraph system, the job of collecting weather observations and issuing storm warnings. This job was considered vital to the nation's defense, because storms could interrupt military activities. The job was later transferred to the U.S. Weather Bureau, now called the National Weather Service.

The modern practice of weather forecasting began in Norway after the end of World War I. There, meteorologists Jakob and Vilhelm Bjerknes, Carl-Gustaf Rossby, and Tor Bergeron laid the foundation for our current understanding of weather patterns, storms, rain, snow, and wind. These scientists applied the laws of mathematics and physics to a growing body of weather data from around the world.

New inventions improved the science of weather forecasting at an astonishing rate. **Radar**, a system that uses radio

Poor Richard, 1733.

AN
Almanack

For the Year of Christ

1733,

Being the First after LEAP YEAR.

And makes since the Creation	Years
By the Account of the Eastern *Greeks*	7241
By the Latin Church, when ☉ ent. ♈	6932
By the Computation of *W.W.*	5742
By the *Roman* Chronology	5682
By the *Jewish* Rabbies.	5494

Wherein is contained

The Lunations, Eclipses, Judgment of the Weather, Spring Tides, Planets Motions & mutual Aspects, Sun and Moon's Rising and Setting, Length of Days, Time of High Water, Fairs, Courts, and observable Days.

Fitted to the Latitude of Forty Degrees, and a Meridian of Five Hours West from *London*, but may without sensible Error, serve all the adjacent Places, even from *Newfoundland* to *South-Carolina*

By *RICHARD SAUNDERS*, Philom.

PHILADELPHIA:
Printed and sold by *B. FRANKLIN*, at the New Printing Office near the Market

---

POOR RICHARD'S ALMANAC

Poor Richard's Almanac was first published in December 1732. According to the book's preface, Richard was Richard Saunders, a poor man trying to make money by selling his book. Actually, Richard was the early American leader Benjamin Franklin. Franklin published his almanac for 25 years. It contained essays, poems, recipes, and humor, as well as facts about the weather, tides, planets, medicine, and history. *Poor Richard's Almanac* is still published today, although it is now called the *Old Farmer's Almanac*. It contains a lot of information on weather and climate, although its forecasts are not as accurate as those provided by the National Weather Service.

waves to locate clouds and storms, was developed during World War II. In later years, **satellites**, spacecraft that orbit the Earth, allowed scientists to photograph and measure weather patterns from space. Computers allowed scientists to store and analyze huge amounts of data.

Another milestone in the history of weather forecasting was the invention of the television set. Making its way into millions

The first TV weather reporters gave their predictions using a variety of gimmicks, including live animals, puppets, and poems: "Rain today and rain tonight, tomorrow still more rain in sight." Creative forecasters said things like "unidentified frying objects" and "uncomfortable as a swordfish with an ingrown nose." They made up new words such as "fozzle" (fog and drizzle), "pleezy" (pleasant and breezy), and "snirt" (snow and dirt) to describe outdoor conditions. Sometimes forecasters even stood on their heads!

Funny forecaster Sonny ▶ Eliot

This balloon carries scientific instruments that will measure weather conditions high above the ground.

of American homes in the 1950s, television made weather forecasts a part of everyday life. People could watch weather reports on the evening news, just as we do today.

The weather is very complicated and difficult to predict, and people sometimes criticize weather forecasters when their predictions aren't correct. Some people even blame forecasters for bad weather that they predicted correctly! On the positive side, though, weather forecasters can work with vast amounts of information. Thousands of weather observations and measurements are collected all over the world every day. The more information a meteorologist has, the better the chance of an accurate forecast.

This book will help you understand how meteorologists observe, analyze, and forecast the weather. You'll learn about weather patterns, weather maps, and forecasting tools. You'll also learn to build your own weather station, keep a weather log, even make your own forecasts. With practice, you may be able to predict the next school closing!

1
WEATHER BASICS

If we're going to learn how meteorologists predict the weather, we first have to know how the weather works. The word weather refers to the condition of the **atmosphere** at a specific time and place. The atmosphere is the invisible blanket of air that surrounds the Earth.

Water and the Air

What is air exactly? Air is a mixture of invisible gases, mostly nitrogen (more than 75 percent) and oxygen (more than 20 percent). Hundreds of other gases are also present in air, but in much smaller amounts. These other gases include carbon dioxide, which helps trap heat near the Earth, and ozone, which protects plants and animals from harmful energy from the Sun.

Another important gas found in the air is **water vapor**—water in gas form. Depending upon where you live, between 1 and 4 percent of the air is made up of water vapor. These numbers may seem small. But water vapor in the air is responsible for supplying clouds, rain, and snow to all parts of the Earth.

Water vapor forms when liquid water turns into a gas. The name of this process is **evaporation** and it is caused by heat. Even a slight amount of heat will cause water to evaporate. But water evaporates most quickly at high temperatures. Most of the water vapor in the air is produced when the Sun's powerful heat evaporates water at the surface of the oceans.

The amount of water vapor in the air is called the **relative humidity**. People often feel uncomfortable when the relative humidity is either very high or very low. On hot summer days

Rain comes from water vapor in the air.

with high relative humidity, people often complain that the air feels "muggy" or "sticky." High relative humidity makes sweat stick to our skin. Low relative humidity dries our skin, making it feel itchy and chapped.

Relative humidity is always expressed as a percentage. "Thirty percent relative humidity" means that the air contains 30 percent of the water vapor that it can possibly hold. The amount of water vapor air can hold depends on air temperature. Cold air cannot hold as much water vapor as warm air can. So, during winter, the air often feels dry, even when the relative humidity is high.

Deserts often have clear skies and low relative humidity.

Relative humidity is important to weather forecasters because it tells them if the air holds enough moisture (water vapor) for clouds to form. When the relative humidity is low, as it often is in the desert, the skies are usually cloudless. When the relative humidity is as high as it can possibly be—100 percent—clouds will form.

Cloudy Skies

Clouds are collections of microscopic water droplets (and sometimes ice crystals) that float in the air. Clouds form when water vapor changes from a gas back into liquid water. The name of this process is **condensation**.

Condensation is the opposite of evaporation. Whereas evaporation occurs when air heats up, condensation occurs when air cools down. Air cools as it rises high into the atmosphere—several miles above the ground—where temperatures are often very low.

Higher temperatures near the ground might cause air to rise, because warm air rises. Or moving air (wind) might rise when it flows over high hills or mountains. In both cases, the rising air will cool, and water vapor in the air will condense—turn into tiny liquid water droplets. These droplets will cluster together and form clouds.

Clouds are often a sign of the weather to come and are thus key to forecasting the weather. Once you learn to recognize different types of clouds, it's a good idea to look at the sky and identify the clouds every day. Before long, you'll be forecasting the weather yourself.

Clouds are named by their shape and by their height above the ground. *Cumulus* clouds form less than a mile above the ground. They are white and puffy and often form on warm afternoons. Cumulus clouds that form higher in the atmosphere, between about 1 and 3 miles above the ground, are called *altocumulus* ("alto" means high). Cumulus and altocumulus clouds are about the same size. But altocumulus clouds look smaller because they're farther away.

Sometimes cumulus clouds grow into towering *cumulonimbus* clouds, also called thunderstorms. *Nimbus* means rainstorm in Latin. Spotting cumulonimbus clouds is a good way to predict the weather, because these clouds often bring rain, thunder, and lightning.

Stratus clouds are gray and gloomy. They form in layers that may cover the sky as far as you can see. These clouds look dark because they block out light from the Sun. Stratus clouds that produce rain or snow are called *nimbostratus* clouds. Stratus clouds that form between 1 and 3 miles above the ground are called *altostratus* clouds. To tell the difference between altostratus and stratus clouds, look for the Sun. You won't see it through a stratus cloud. But you'll see the Sun as a circle of weak light shining through an altostratus cloud.

Cirrus clouds form at least 3 miles above the ground, where temperatures are very low. Whereas cumulus and stratus clouds are made up mostly of water droplets, cirrus clouds are made of ice crystals—frozen water droplets. Cirrus clouds are white and can take on many different appearances: sometimes they are feathery and delicate, sometimes they are flat and layered.

Cumulus clouds (above) can grow into cumulonimbus clouds (below), also known as thunderstorms.

Wispy white clouds (above) are called cirrus clouds. Stratus clouds (right) blanket the sky.

Cirrus clouds that form in patches or clumps are called *cirrocumulus* clouds. Cirrus clouds that form in layers are called *cirrostratus* clouds. Cirrostratus clouds often give the sky a milky white color and create a colorful halo (a ring of light) around the Sun or Moon. These clouds are often a sign of approaching rain or snow. We'll learn why a little later.

Fog is a special type of cloud, one that forms near the ground. Fog often forms in coastal areas, when warm, moist air from the ocean blows over cooler land. When the air reaches the land and cools, water vapor in the air condenses, forming a cloud that people can walk right through—fog!

Showers and Snowflakes

Clouds are responsible for another important weather event: **precipitation**. Precipitation, a word used to describe any kind of rain or snow, is something that many of us spend a lot of time thinking about: whether or not to wear a raincoat, whether the streets will be icy, whether school will be canceled because of snow.

Precipitation occurs when water droplets floating within clouds combine and become so heavy that the air can no longer hold them. Most precipitation, even during the summer, begins as snow. High in the atmosphere, the air is very cold—often well below 32° F, the temperature at which water freezes. As a result, clouds that form high in the atmosphere contain lots of tiny ice crystals.

As these ice crystals stick together, they grow heavier and heavier and might begin to fall. Then we call them snowflakes.

If the air near the ground is cold (as it often is in winter), the snowflakes will stay frozen as they fall to Earth. If the temperature near the ground is high enough (above 32°F), the snowflakes will melt and form raindrops.

When raindrops are very small, they're called drizzle or mist. Rainfall that starts and stops suddenly is called a shower. Thunderstorms bring heavy rains, high winds, and lightning. Thunderstorms are often accompanied by hailstones, clumps of frozen raindrops that can be larger than 2 inches across. Large

DEW POINT

The dew point is the temperature at which condensation occurs—the temperature at which air can no longer hold its moisture. On a clear night, air near the ground sometimes cools to the dew point temperature. Water vapor in the air condenses (turns into tiny drops of liquid water), and a blanket of glistening dew forms on the ground. If the dew point temperature is below 32°F, ice crystals—called frost—might form.

Dew drops on a spider web ▶

A nighttime thunderstorm

hailstones can be very dangerous. Imagine how much damage might be caused by 2-inch chunks of ice falling from the sky! The most severe thunderstorms can bring tornadoes, intense swirling winds, spinning as fast as 200 miles per hour.

Snowfall comes in different forms too. Light snow falling for a short time is called snow flurries or snow showers. A severe winter storm with drifting and blowing snow is called a blizzard.

LAKE EFFECT SNOW

The downwind shores of large lakes, such as the Great Lakes, receive more snowfall than surrounding areas do. Here's why. Water cools more slowly than land does, so in the winter, lakes stay warmer than land. As wind blows over a warm lake, the air warms up and takes on water vapor from the lake. As the air passes back over land, it cools quickly. Because there's so much water vapor in the air, clouds form and snow falls.

Precipitation is sometimes a mixture of both rain and snow. Some examples of mixed precipitation are sleet, ice pellets, and freezing rain.

Season to Season

How do you know what kind of weather to expect? Will your region have thunderstorms today? A blizzard? Sunshine? One basic way to predict the weather is to understand the seasons: winter, spring, summer, and fall (autumn).

The seasons are created by the tilt of the Earth as it circles the Sun. The Northern Hemisphere, north of the equator, tilts toward the Sun during summer and away from the Sun in winter. This pattern creates the seasonal weather familiar to most Americans—cold winters (often with snow); warm, sunny springs; hot summers; and cool, rainy autumns.

You've got to consider more than just the seasons to predict the weather, though. Geographic features—mountains, oceans, and deserts—also influence the weather. Coastal areas are often humid because they're near large bodies of water. Deserts tend to be dry. Places near the North and South poles are usually very cold. The word **climate** refers to the *typical* weather found in a region.

Even though each region and each season has its typical weather, the weather still changes from day to day. Air is always moving, and moving air means changing weather. In the next chapter, we'll learn about moving air, commonly called wind.

2

AIR ON THE MOVE

The atmosphere is always in motion. Air is constantly rising, sinking, and moving horizontally (sideways) across the Earth's surface. Moving air brings different kinds of weather to all parts of the globe. Why does air move? The answer is **air pressure**.

Pressure is created whenever force is applied to one or more objects. When you kick a football, for example, your foot puts pressure on the football, causing it to fly through the air. In the atmosphere, pressure is caused by the force of gravity pressing air against the Earth's surface.

Pressure is connected to temperature, the measure of heat. When one changes, so does the other. You can see this connection yourself by putting your football (if you haven't kicked it too far) in the refrigerator for a few minutes. When you take the ball out of the refrigerator, you'll find that the air pressure inside the football has dropped. The ball appears to be deflated. After the ball warms up for a few minutes, the air pressure will increase, restoring the ball to its original shape. In this experiment, falling temperatures cause pressure to drop.

24

When the pressure in two places is not the same, air will begin to move. Moving air is called wind. ▶

AIR PRESSURE

Place a paint stick on the edge of a table, with the end of the stick reaching a few inches over the edge. Slap the overhanging end of the stick and the other end will jump up.

Now spread a piece of newspaper over the part of the stick that is resting on the table. When you slap the overhanging end again, the stick won't jump up. Air pressure is holding the newspaper and the paint stick down.

The weight of the newspaper isn't holding the stick down. You can prove this by crumpling the paper into a ball and placing it on the stick. When you slap the overhanging end again, both the stick and the ball of newspaper will jump up. The weight of the paper is not great enough to hold the stick down. It is air pressure, pushing down on the spread-out newspaper, that keeps the stick from jumping.

The atmosphere behaves a little differently than a football in the refrigerator, though. In the atmosphere, *rising* temper-atures generally cause pressure to drop. This effect is due to the fact that warm air rises and cold air sinks. When warm air rises, less air presses against the ground, so air pressure de-creases. Cold temperatures cause air pressure to *increase.* Cold air sinks, meaning that more air presses against the ground when it's cold.

When the air pressure in two places is not the same, air will begin to move. To understand the relationship between pressure and air movement (wind), imagine a block of wood resting on the floor. If you put pressure on the block by pushing it with your hand, the block will begin to move. It moves because the pressure on one side of the block is greater than the pressure on the other side.

Winds

Like a block of wood, air will move when pressure in two places is not equal. Why is air pressure different from place to place? The answer is temperature. If you've ever spent any time along a lake or ocean shoreline, you've probably experienced firsthand the connection between temperature, air pressure, and air movement. It's often windy along a shoreline, especially if the Sun is shining brightly. Let's examine why.

Land warms up faster than water does, so the shore usually becomes warmer than the water on a sunny day. As air over the land warms and rises, air pressure drops. The air over the water is cooler, so it sinks. Air pressure over the water rises. Under high pressure, the air over the water will begin to move. A cool wind, called a sea breeze, will blow from the water toward the land.

This same connection between temperature and air pressure creates the **prevailing winds**, powerful wind belts that circle the Earth. As sunlight heats the Earth, certain areas get warmer than others. The tropics, near the equator, get quite hot. The

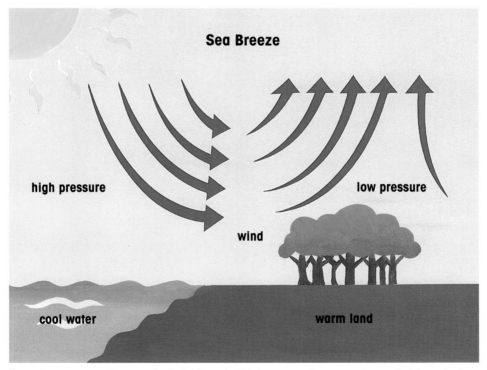

On a hot summer day, we find sinking air (high pressure) over water and rising air (low pressure) over land. The air under high pressure moves toward the area where the pressure is lower, creating the sea breeze (or the "lake breeze" on the shores of large lakes).

WIND CHILL

Low temperature is not the only weather feature that makes us feel cold. Wind also cools us down by taking away our body heat. The combination of low temperature and wind is called wind chill. Suppose the wind is blowing at 15 miles per hour and the air temperature is 20°F. The temperature you feel—the wind chill equivalent—will be -5°F. On a cold day, use the following chart to find the wind chill equivalent.

		Air Temperature (degrees Fahrenheit)						
		20	**15**	**10**	**5**	**0**	**-5**	**-10**
	5	16	11	6	0	-5	-10	-15
Wind	**10**	3	-3	-9	-15	-22	-27	-34
speed	**15**	-5	-11	-18	-25	-31	-38	-45
(mph)	**20**	-10	-17	-24	-31	-39	-46	-53
	25	-15	-22	-29	-36	-44	-51	-59
	30	-18	-25	-33	-41	-49	-56	-64

North and South poles remain cold. Since warm air rises and puts less pressure on the Earth than cold air does, we often find low pressure over warm areas and high pressure over cold areas.

Air under high pressure moves toward places where the pressure is lower. This movement, combined with the Earth's daily rotation, creates the prevailing winds: the *trade winds* near the equator, the *polar easterlies* near the North and South poles, and the *prevailing westerlies* between the poles and the equator.

Winds are important to weather forecasters. Suppose the temperature in Detroit is 74°F, and the wind is blowing from the west. Suppose the temperature in Chicago, 300 miles west of Detroit, is 52°F. Because the wind is blowing from the west, we can predict that the cool air in Chicago will soon reach Detroit. Our forecast: falling temperatures over Detroit.

Pressure Systems

Air pressure is also important to weather forecasters. A large area under either high or low pressure is called a **pressure system**. Pressure systems can be as big as 2,000 miles across. The systems move slowly across large regions, changing the weather as they go.

High pressure systems, sometimes called highs, have high pressure in the middle of the system and low pressure on the edges. **Low pressure systems**, or lows, have low pressure in the middle and high pressure on the edges. The high and low pressure are caused mainly by differences in temperature.

Winds circle around both high and low pressure systems. In the Northern Hemisphere (north of the equator), wind flows around high pressure systems in a clockwise direction and around low pressure systems in a counterclockwise direction. In the Southern Hemisphere, the directions are opposite: highs rotate counterclockwise and lows rotate clockwise. Let's examine what happens in both kinds of pressure systems.

In a low, the lowest pressure is located in the middle of the system. As wind blows around the low, some air from the high pressure areas on the outside will move toward the low pressure area in the center of the system, creating a "pile up" of air. Pretty soon this growing pile of air begins to overflow—it is forced to rise. As we've already learned, rising air will cool, create clouds, and possibly bring rain and snow. Low pressure systems, therefore, often bring stormy weather.

In a high pressure system, on the other hand, low pressure is found away from the center of the system, along the outside edges. As wind blows around the high, some air will move from the high pressure area in the center of the system toward the low pressure area on the outside. This movement causes a kind of "hole" to form in the center of the high. But because the atmosphere is constantly in motion, the hole always gets filled with more air. Where does the air come from? The hole gets filled with sinking air from above. Since air in a high sinks rather than rises, clouds and precipitation are unlikely to form there. Instead, highs usually bring clear skies and sunshine.

If the air pressure in your region is decreasing, a low pressure system may be headed your way. Meteorologists call this decrease a "falling barometer," because pressure is measured with an instrument called a **barometer**. This forecast doesn't

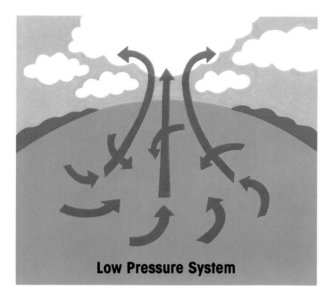

Air in a low pressure system rises, creating clouds and precipitation.

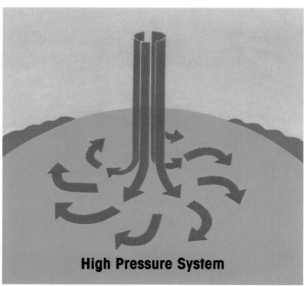

Air in a high pressure system sinks, leaving clear skies.

Two low pressure systems over the Bering Sea, photographed from the space shuttle *Discovery*. Note the spinning motion of the clouds in each system.

mean that barometers are going to fall from the sky, but it does mean that clouds and precipitation may be coming. A "rising barometer," on the other hand, usually means that higher pressure, sinking air, and clear skies are on the way.

Air Masses

A simple weather forecasting technique goes like this: "the weather tomorrow will be the same as the weather today." This technique is called the "persistence method." While it is not terribly accurate, it does have some merit.

The weather often stays the same for a few days at a time. If you've ever spent a winter in the northern United States, you know that three or four days of extreme cold might be followed by several days of warmer temperatures and possibly snow, followed by a return to colder conditions.

The weather feature often responsible for this pattern is the air mass. An **air mass** is a large body of air, with roughly the same temperature and relative humidity throughout the whole mass. Like a pressure system, an air mass might be several thousand miles across. One air mass might even cover the whole continental United States.

An air mass forms when a large high pressure system lingers over a region for several days or more. As air rotates around and around the center of the high, it rubs against the Earth below. If the Earth is wet (as it is in the ocean), a lot of water will evaporate—turn into water vapor. A moist air mass will form. Drier air masses form over land, where much less water is found. Air masses can be either warm or cold, depending on the temperature of the Earth below. They slowly move, bringing heat waves, cold snaps, and other weather events to the places they go.

There are four main types of air masses. *Continental polar* air masses form over snow-covered lands, such as Alaska and northern Canada. Because they form near polar regions, these air masses are cold. And because they form over land, not water, they are dry (have low relative humidity). They bring clear skies, occasionally with scattered cumulus clouds. They can bring bitter cold temperatures in winter and cool weather in summer.

Maritime polar air masses form over the northern Atlantic and Pacific oceans. Like continental polar air masses, they bring cool air. But because they form over the ocean, these air masses are moist (have high relative humidity). They bring rain, snow, and fog. Maritime polar air masses often travel over the East and West coasts of the United States.

Maritime tropical air masses form near the equator—in the Gulf of Mexico, the Caribbean Sea, the eastern Pacific Ocean, and other tropical waters. Since they form in hot regions, these air masses are warm. And since they form over the ocean, they are moist. They can bring hot, humid air and thunderstorms in summer and heavy snowfall in winter.

Continental tropical air masses form over deserts during the summer. They are hot and dry. They bring clear skies, hot weather, and sometimes drought. Continental tropical air masses are common in the southwestern United States.

If you know that an air mass is coming to your area, you can use your knowledge to make a weather forecast. Just remember the following combinations: continental—dry, maritime—wet, tropical—hot, polar—cold. Air masses usually stay in one place for three to five days. So you'll have a pretty good idea what type of weather is in store for the next few days—until the next air mass moves in.

Fronts

Shortly after the end of World War I (1918), meteorologist Jakob Bjerknes pioneered the modern practice of weather forecasting in Norway. Because Bjerknes and his coworkers had been trained in the army, they used a military term to describe another important weather event: the **front**.

Whereas a military front is the boundary between opposing armies in battle, a weather front is the boundary between two air masses. When one air mass moves in and another one leaves, drastic weather changes often occur at the boundary. At a front we might see changes in temperature, relative humidity, clouds, wind, precipitation, or everything all at once. You might say that air masses engage in a battle along the weather front.

There are four types of weather fronts. Two of them, the **cold front** and the **warm front**, are named after the temperature of the approaching air mass. When a continental polar air mass approaches and bumps into a maritime tropical air mass, for instance, a cold front forms at the boundary. When a warm air mass approaches and collides with a cold air mass, a warm front forms. As you might expect, cold fronts bring falling temperatures. Warm fronts bring rising temperatures. In the United States (and other parts of the Northern Hemisphere), cold fronts usually come from the north or northwest and warm fronts come from the south or southwest.

Cold fronts generally move faster than warm fronts. Sometimes, a fast-moving cold front will overtake a slower moving warm front, producing an **occluded front**. The fourth kind of weather front, the **stationary front**, forms when two air masses move side-by-side without pushing into each other. Each type of front causes a special weather pattern as it passes through a region.

Whenever cold air and warm air meet, clouds are likely to form. That's because warm air rises and cold air sinks. So warm air will rise over cold air at a front. The rising air will cool, water vapor will condense, and clouds will form.

At cold fronts, where cold air bumps into warm air, warm

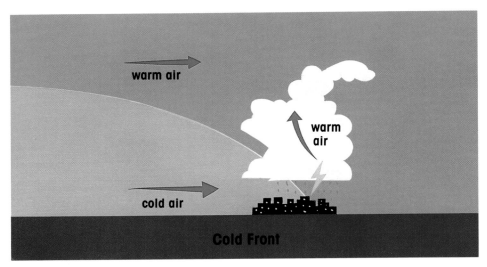

At a cold front, air rises very quickly, producing heavy storms.

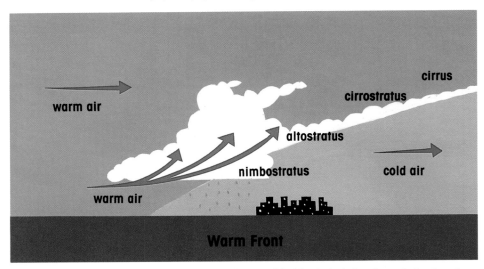

At a warm front, air rises more slowly, creating a wide blanket of clouds and steady rain or snow showers.

air rises very quickly. This quick rising action can create large cumulus and cumulonimbus clouds, sudden thunderstorms in summer, and heavy snowfalls in winter. Gusty winds, falling temperatures, and decreasing humidity also accompany cold fronts.

Air rises more slowly at warm fronts. Along a warm front, the approaching warm air mass slides gradually over the cold air mass, creating a wide blanket of clouds that can bring steady and prolonged rain or snow. Warm fronts also bring winds from the south or southwest (in the Northern Hemisphere), higher temperatures, and increased humidity.

A special cloud pattern accompanies the warm front. The clouds start out high in the sky and get lower nearer to the front. Cirrus clouds are found ahead of the front, changing to cirrostratus, then altostratus, and finally nimbostratus at the front itself. Occluded fronts and stationary fronts contain a combination of cold-front and warm-front weather features.

Suppose gusty winds begin to blow from the north and dark thunderstorm clouds loom on the horizon. Chances are, a cold front is approaching your region. You can expect brief and sudden precipitation within the next few hours.

Cold fronts are found at the edge of an approaching cold air mass, so you can also predict falling temperatures. Furthermore, since you know that air masses are very large, you can predict that the lower temperatures will be around for a few more days, until the next front comes along. Now you're beginning to forecast the weather yourself.

3

SKY WATCHING

In the days before TV and radio weather forecasts, people often used rhymes and legends to help them predict the weather. Most of these sayings and tales weren't very accurate.

A good example is the story of Groundhog Day. According to legend, on the second day of February, the furry rodent comes out of its hole and looks around. If the groundhog sees its shadow, winter will last six more weeks. If not, spring will come early. Despite the popular appeal of the story (a town in Pennsylvania keeps a pet groundhog just to make the prediction), weather records have proven the groundhog wrong again and again.

But some weather sayings are based in fact and can be quite accurate. Here are some of the more trustworthy ones:

A ring around the Sun or Moon
brings rain or snow upon you soon.

Cirrostratus clouds can create a halo around the Sun, as shown here, or around the Moon.

As you'll remember, cirrostratus clouds often make a halo, a ring of colored light, around the Sun or Moon. The halo is created by ice crystals inside the clouds. When light rays—traveling from the Sun or reflecting off the Moon—pass through the crystals, they change direction. The change in direction creates a halo effect. If you see a halo, then you're looking through cirrostratus clouds. Cirrostratus clouds, when followed by altostratus and nimbostratus clouds, signal the approach of a warm front, which often brings rain or snow.

When high clouds and low clouds do not march together prepare for a blow and a change in the weather.

High clouds and low clouds move in different directions when wind high in the atmosphere blows from a different direction than wind closer to the ground. This wind pattern often signals an approaching air mass or the development of a high or low pressure system—all of which mean changing weather.

> *When windows won't open and salt clogs the shaker*
> *the weather will favor the umbrella-maker.*

High relative humidity can make salt sticky and difficult to pour. High humidity also causes wood to swell, making wooden windows hard to open and close. When the humidity is high, there's a good chance of clouds and rain.

> *If clear be the Moon*
> *frost will come soon.*

Cloudy nights are often warm, because clouds act like a blanket for the Earth, keeping heat near the ground. Clear nights, on the other hand, are usually colder. When skies are clear, you'll get a good look at the Moon after dark, temperatures will fall, and frost might form on the ground.

Reading the Clouds

Air is invisible. Although we can't see air, we can observe its behavior by watching things that float through it. Even if you're not a trained meteorologist, you can observe a lot of telltale signs about the weather to come just by looking at the sky.

"Looks like rain!" Thunderstorms on the horizon

Clouds give some of the most reliable clues about the coming weather. A pattern of high clouds (cirrus) changing to lower clouds (altostratus) changing to still lower clouds (stratus) generally indicates the approach of a warm front. Winds will soon blow from the south or southwest, with increasing temperatures and relative humidity and steady precipitation lasting several hours.

Cumulus clouds that quickly grow into tall cumulonimbus clouds (thunderstorms) may signal the onset of a cold front. If you see cumulonimbus clouds in the distance, you may soon get heavy rain, thunder, and lightning, as well as decreasing temperatures.

Cloud movement, as well as type, is another guide to the weather. When air pressure drops, winds pick up speed. So, if strong winds push clouds quickly across the sky, a low pressure system may be approaching your area.

Look at a smokestack to get more clues about the weather. A smoke plume that loops up and down often signals showers and thunderstorms. The same rising and falling air motions that make the smoke curl and twist also cause air to rise and form clouds. When smoke plumes are flat, there is little rising or sinking motion in the air. So rain clouds, showers, and thunderstorms are unlikely.

Help from the Weather Map

Weather maps will give you more information about the weather than you could ever gather on your own. A weather map is like a road map to the atmosphere. It might contain observations made over a certain part of the country, a whole continent, or even the entire Earth.

Some weather maps are very complicated. Only trained meteorologists use them. Other weather maps, such as those that appear in your newspaper or on television newscasts, are easy to read. Let's look at the types of "road signs" you'll find on the weather map in your newspaper.

Many weather maps use colors to show temperatures in different regions. The map will include a legend, a diagram matching each color to a temperature range. Precipitation symbols are also printed on weather maps. A series of diagonal lines across a certain region might represent rain. A series of small Xs means snow. The legend gives the meaning of each symbol.

After you've looked at temperature and precipitation on your weather map, locate the large weather patterns—pressure

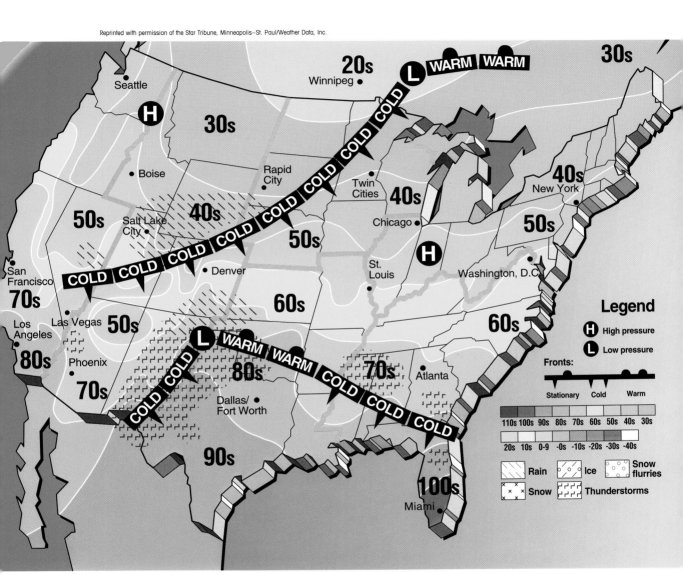

Find your town on the weather map and use the legend to figure out the forecast for your region.

systems and fronts. High and low pressure systems are shown with large H's and L's. Areas under a high are likely to be sunny, and areas under a low are likely to be cloudy.

Fronts are shown on a weather map by a line, with arrows showing which way a cold front is moving and half-circles showing which way a warm front is moving. Stationary fronts and occluded fronts are shown using a combination of the two symbols. Find the fronts on your weather map, and you'll know where to find clouds and precipitation.

Now focus on a particular area—your town, for example. You can use your knowledge of meteorology to determine what the weather is like there and how it may change over the next day or two. If your town is near a front, expect a change in weather. Exactly how your weather will change depends on the type of front that's nearby. Suppose it's summertime and a cold front is approaching. You can expect brief, heavy precipitation (rain showers and maybe a thunderstorm), gusty winds, and falling temperatures.

With an approaching warm front, you can predict increasing temperatures and relative humidity, steady rains lasting up to several hours, and increasing cloudiness. You can even pinpoint the types of clouds to come: first high clouds (cirrus and cirrostratus), then lower clouds (altostratus), and finally nimbostratus.

If your town is near a high pressure system, you'll probably have a sunny day. The position of the high can even tell you which way the winds will blow. Suppose you live in Chicago and you see a large H, a high pressure system, to the south of

FORECASTING TERMS

The National Weather Service has specific definitions for a number of forecasting terms. Listen for these words the next time you hear a weather forecast:

- Mostly Sunny or Mostly Clear: Between $1/10$ and $3/10$ of the sky is covered by clouds.
- Partly Cloudy or Partly Sunny: Between $4/10$ and $6/10$ of the sky is covered by clouds.
- Mostly Cloudy or Considerable Cloudiness: Between $7/10$ and $8/10$ of the sky is covered by clouds.
- Cloudy: More than $9/10$ of the sky is covered by clouds.
- Fair: Used to describe nighttime conditions. Less than $4/10$ of the sky is covered by clouds, there are no strong winds, no precipitation, and no extreme temperatures.
- Variable Cloudiness: Irregular conditions with an increase or decrease in cloudiness several times during the forecast period.

CRITICAL INFORMATION

Many businesses and organizations rely on accurate weather forecasts. Airports and pilots need detailed information about wind speed, cloud conditions, visibility, and the location of storms. If bad weather is predicted, flights might be cancelled or routes changed. Boaters need to know about storms and winds that can create dangerous waves at sea. Farmers use rainfall and snowfall forecasts when they are preparing to plant and harvest crops. Even the military uses weather forecasts to plan troop movements and air and sea missions.

The National Weather Service runs special radio stations that give weather forecasts round-the-clock. These forecasts are more detailed than those given on television or in the newspaper. They are useful to farmers, boaters, scientists, and amateur sky watchers. The National Weather Service and the Federal Aviation Administration also run weather radar systems and radio stations just for pilots.

Radar stations like this one detect clouds and storms several hundred miles away.

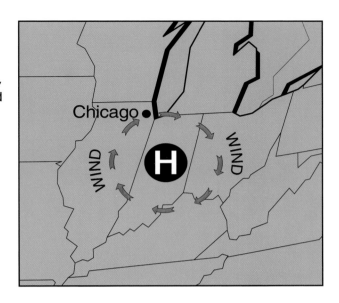

In the Northern Hemisphere, winds blow clockwise around a high.

Chicago on your weather map. Expect winds from the southwest, since winds blow clockwise around highs in the Northern Hemisphere.

Besides printing a map of the nation, newspapers usually include a chart, listing high and low temperatures for big cities in the United States and around the world. The chart includes yesterday's and today's readings and predictions for tomorrow. This information helps travelers decide whether to pack their long underwear, their raincoats, or their suntan lotion. Newspapers give extra details about state and local weather, such as snowfall totals, temperature readings, and predictions for the coming week. Television weather forecasts give similar information. Where does all this information come from? That's the topic of our next chapter.

4

PROFESSIONAL FORECASTING

The National Weather Service, along with similar organizations in other countries, monitors weather around the clock. At thousands of weather stations around the world, every one to three hours, meteorologists take ground-level measurements of air pressure, temperature, relative humidity, wind speed, wind direction, clouds, precipitation, and visibility (the distance you can see outside). Meteorologists make these measurements using a variety of instruments.

Forecasting Tools

As we learned in Chapter Two, air pressure is measured with a barometer. Air pressure readings are usually listed in "inches of mercury," because many barometers contain a tube of liquid mercury. As air presses upon the mercury, it rises and falls in the tube, depending on the degree of pressure.

Temperature is measured by a **thermometer** and is recorded either in degrees Fahrenheit or degrees Celsius. On the Fahrenheit scale, water freezes at 32° and boils at 212°. On the Celsius scale, water freezes at 0° and boils at 100°. The most common thermometers contain a sealed tube of mercury or another liquid. The liquid rises and falls in the tube, responding to changes in temperature.

A **hygrometer** records relative humidity. Some hygrometers measure how quickly water evaporates at a specific temperature. Others measure the weight of moisture in the air. Some hygrometers even use human hair, which increases in length as moisture in the air increases.

Wind speed is measured by an **anemometer**, a device that rotates faster and faster as wind speed increases. A **weather vane** turns with the wind to indicate wind direction.

A **rain gauge** is used to record rainfall. Most rain gauges measure either the height of rainwater collecting in a tube or the weight of rainwater collecting in a bucket.

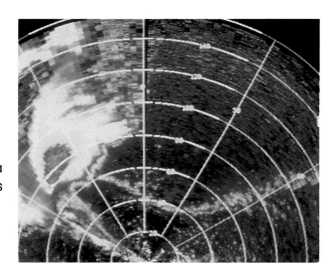

A thunderstorm shown on a radar screen. The red area is the center of the storm.

Releasing a radiosonde into the sky at an Alaskan weather station

Meteorologists measure snowfall simply by placing a measuring stick in the snow. But since wind can blow snow into big drifts, meteorologists take snowfall readings in at least three different places in one area. Then they average the measurements.

Forecasters at the National Weather Service use advanced equipment to record certain aspects of the weather that can't be measured with the basic equipment listed above. Radar systems send out radio waves that bounce off falling raindrops and snowflakes inside clouds. The systems then analyze the returning signals, or echoes, and map the location and movement of clouds and storms. Radar can detect storms up to 250 miles away.

An advanced type of radar, **Doppler radar**, not only locates storms but also measures wind speed. The system is especially useful for locating powerful thunderstorms and tornadoes and for determining their strength. Doppler radar compares the frequency (rate) of outgoing radio waves with the frequency of returning radio waves. The greater the variation between the outgoing and incoming signals, the faster a storm is moving.

Radiosondes, groups of weather instruments attached to hydrogen-filled balloons, measure weather conditions above the ground, up to 10 miles in the air. Radiosondes are equipped with radio transmitters that send the measurements back to meteorologists on the ground.

Instruments aboard satellites measure and photograph the atmosphere from thousands of miles above the Earth. In addition to measuring conditions over land, satellites monitor clouds and weather patterns over the oceans, where few ground-level measurements are made. Special airplanes and ships at sea also measure weather conditions in remote places.

Once gathered, all weather observations and measurements made in the United States are immediately sent by communications satellite to the National Meteorological Center (part of the National Weather Service) in Camp Springs, Maryland. Information from weather stations outside the United States is sent there as well. Meteorologists will use this information to make their predictions.

A Two-Step Process

Weather forecasting is a two-step process. The first step, the diagnosis, involves gathering information about the current conditions of the atmosphere. The forecaster does this by examining weather maps, satellite photographs, radar images, and other weather data provided by the National Meteorological Center. The second step is the prognosis, or prediction. In this step, the forecaster applies the principles of meteorology to the present conditions of the atmosphere and then predicts how the weather might change.

Meteorologists use a variety of skills to make these predictions, including old-fashioned sky watching. Experience is also important. A veteran forecaster may remember a weather pattern from previous years and use his or her knowledge of past events to make an accurate prediction the next time.

But even experienced weather forecasters use words such as "maybe," "a chance of," and "probable." Meteorologists are

JOBS IN METEOROLOGY

Most meteorologists are weather forecasters. Forecasters work at National Weather Service offices throughout the country, at television and radio stations, and at universities. Other meteorologists work for the military, federal and state government, farm agencies, and private industry. Many meteorologists focus on a specific subject, such as hurricanes or air pollution. Most of the jobs require a college degree in meteorology or a related area of science.

sometimes criticized for not being certain about the weather. Comedians joke that "meteorology is the only field in which you can be wrong half the time and still keep your job." In reality, meteorology is a quickly improving science, and weather forecasts are correct much more than half the time.

In recent years, meteorologists have had help in making their forecasts from supercomputers operated by the National Meteorological Center. The computers use complex mathematical formulas to create special weather maps. The maps, used mainly by meteorologists, show weather conditions around the world and make predictions for several days into the future. The computers use the familiar two-step forecasting process. Worldwide weather observations provide the diagnosis, and computer programs make the prognosis.

Every 12 hours, the National Meteorological Center distributes the maps to National Weather Service offices, television and radio stations, newspapers, universities, and foreign weather organizations. Forecasters use these maps, along with their own observations and knowledge of weather patterns, to create their forecasts.

Despite great improvements in the science of meteorology, weather forecasting will never be perfectly accurate. Many aspects of the weather are still not well understood. Tornadoes and hurricanes are good examples. Meteorologists understand a lot about *why* these fierce storms form. But they are not yet able to predict *where* the storms will form. Another obstacle to accurate forecasting stems from incomplete information. Although weather measurements are taken every one to three

Using weather maps and computer-generated graphics provided by the National Meteorological Center, a scientist prepares the local forecast.

hours at thousands of stations around the world, a lot of weather goes unseen and unmeasured between stations. Weather that is not observed cannot be diagnosed. Similarly, radiosondes record weather conditions high in the atmosphere only once every 12 hours. A lot can happen in 12 hours—conditions may change and go unrecorded. Although satellites, supercomputers, and other instruments can help meteorologists improve their forecasts, meteorologists will never achieve perfect accuracy.

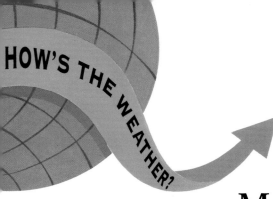

5.

MAKE YOUR OWN WEATHER STATION

You can build instruments that measure air pressure, temperature, humidity, wind speed, wind direction, and precipitation. Follow the instructions to create your own weather station.

Barometer

Materials needed: small glass jar, large uninflated balloon, rubber band, tape, index card, glue, toothpick, pencil.

Instructions: Cut the neck off the balloon. Stretch the remaining part of the balloon over the glass jar and secure it with the rubber band. Tape the index card to the side of the jar and glue the toothpick to the center of the balloon. Make an air pressure scale on the index card by marking "high" above the point of the toothpick and "low" below. Keep your barometer in a cool, dry place, away from direct sunlight.

Explanation: You've just built an instrument known as an aneroid barometer. When the air pressure is high, air will press down on the balloon and cause the toothpick to point up toward

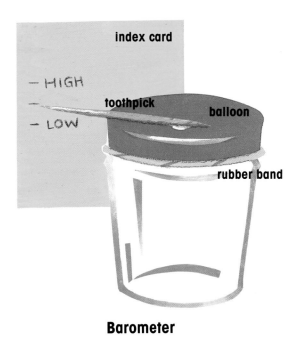

Barometer

▲ What the professionals use:
a mercury barometer

the "high" mark. When the air pressure is low, air inside the jar will push up against the balloon, causing the toothpick to point down toward the "low" mark.

You can make your pressure scale more accurate by listening to a weather forecast and writing the official air pressure reading next to the place on the card where the toothpick points that day. Do this once a day for a week, and you'll have several set points to use as an accurate scale for air pressure.

Thermometer

Accurate temperature measurements require a high-quality glass thermometer. These are inexpensive and are available at most hardware stores. Store-bought thermometers can be dangerous, however, because they are made of glass and can break.

In addition, many glass thermometers contain mercury, a highly toxic substance. Be very careful when handling a glass thermometer. Here's how to build a safe thermometer without glass or mercury.

Materials needed: clear plastic bottle with a plastic cap, modeling clay, clear plastic straw, tape, cardboard, a pitcher of ice water, food coloring

Instructions: Make a hole in the plastic cap. Ask a parent or teacher to drill the hole or pound it for you with a large nail and a hammer. Fill the bottle with ice-cold water and add several drops of food coloring. Make sure you fill the bottle right up to the very top. Now screw on the plastic cap and insert the straw (about one inch) through the hole in the bottle cap. Spread modeling clay around the top of the cap so that the straw stays in place and water cannot spill out around the straw. Tape a thin strip of cardboard to the straw.

Explanation: You've created a simple version of the more familiar store-bought thermometer. Glass thermometers contain a supply of liquid and a thin tube just like your straw. Liquids expand when they're heated, meaning the molecules within them spread out. So when the temperature goes up, the water in your homemade thermometer will expand and travel up the straw. When the temperature drops, the water will sink down inside the straw. You can mark levels on the cardboard strip to record the temperature at different places and times. Remember that your homemade thermometer won't work when the temperature is below 32° F, because the water inside the bottle will freeze.

clear straw

tape

modeling clay

ice water

Thermometer

EXTRA EFFORT

You can use your thermometer to compare temperatures in different parts of your house. Is it warmer in the direct sunshine or in the shade? In the basement or in the attic? You can make a scale by comparing the water levels on your thermometer with temperature readings on a store-bought thermometer.

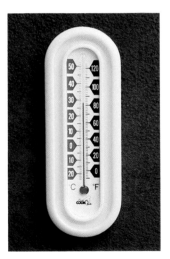

▲ A common household thermometer measures temperature using both the Fahrenheit and Celsius scales.

Hygrometer

Materials needed: cardboard, two thumbtacks, a strand of human hair at least 10 inches long.

Instructions: Cut out a square of cardboard, about 12 inches by 12 inches. Cut a pointer, about 6 inches long, out of another piece of cardboard. Use a thumbtack to poke two small holes, one above the other, in the flat end of the pointer. Tie one end of the hair through the lower hole. Push a thumbtack through the upper hole to attach the pointer to the top left corner of the big cardboard square. Tie the other end of the hair to the remaining thumbtack and push the tack into the cardboard square below the pointer. Make sure the hair is stretched out so that the pointer points straight to the right. Write "low" above the tip of the point and "high" below it.

Explanation: Your instrument is called a hair hygrometer. When the relative humidity is high, the hair will stretch out and the pointer will drop downward. When relative humidity is low, the hair will contract (shrink), and the pointer will move up.

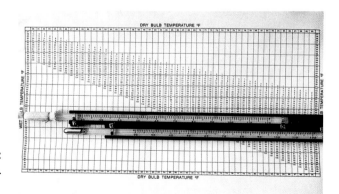

What the professionals use: a psychrometer, a type of hygrometer

60

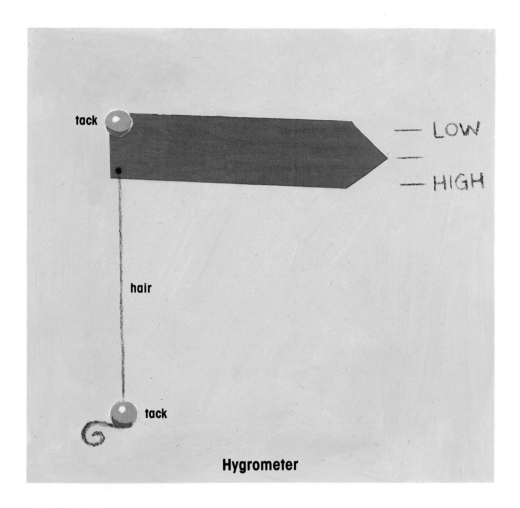

Hygrometer

EXTRA EFFORT

You can observe changes in relative humidity by placing your hygrometer in different places. Try putting it in the refrigerator. Put it in the bathroom when you're taking a bath or shower. You can make a scale by comparing the pointer levels to the official relative humidity reported on a television or radio weather broadcast.

What the professionals use: an aerovane at a California airport. Because weather is so important to aviators, many weather stations ar located at airports. The aerovane holds both an anemometer and a weather vane.

Anemometer

Materials needed: plastic straw, three paper cups, a heavy paper plate, a nail with a narrow head, a nail with a wide head, a square wooden board (about 6 inches by 6 inches), paint or a marker.

Instructions: With the help of a parent or teacher, pound the nail with the narrow head into the center of the board, making sure that it sticks up at least 2 inches. Use paint or a marker to make one cup a different color than the others. Staple the cups to the edge of the paper plate, equal distances apart, so that the open ends all face the same way going around the circle. Place the straw over the nail and balance the plate with cups on the top end of the straw. Carefully push the nail with a wide head through the center of the plate and into the top end of the straw.

Explanation: When the wind blows, air will blow into the open ends of the cups and push the plate around. You can measure the wind speed by counting how many times the colored cup spins around in one minute.

EXTRA EFFORT

You can develop an accurate scale for your anemometer, but you'll need some help from your parents, their car, and a friend. Choose a day with no wind, and ask your parent to take you for a drive on a side street without much traffic. Have your parent drive the car at exactly 5 miles per hour. While the car is moving, carefully hold your anemometer out the window so that the plate can spin. Your friend can count the number of times the plate spins in one minute and write down the outcome. Do the same thing at speeds of 10 and 15 miles per hour. When you're finished, you'll know exactly how many times the plate should spin when your anemometer is standing still and the wind is blowing at 5, 10, and 15 miles an hour.

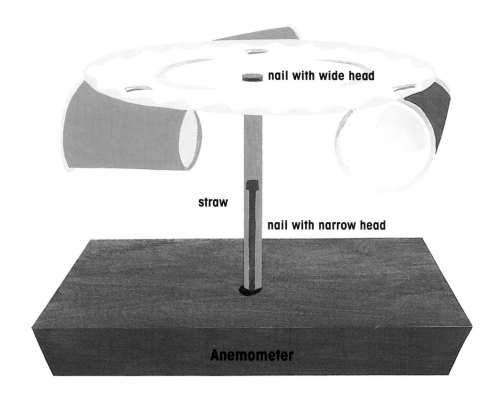

nail with wide head

straw

nail with narrow head

Anemometer

Weather Vane

Materials needed: a directional compass, a square wooden board (about 6 inches by 6 inches), a nail with a narrow head, cardboard, a straw, a pencil, and a stapler.

Instructions: With the help of an adult, pound the nail into the center of the board, making sure that it sticks up at least 2 inches. Cut a pointer, about 6 inches long, out of cardboard. Staple the middle of the pointer to one end of the straw. Place the other end of the straw over the nail sticking out of the board. Using your pencil, mark "North," "East," "West," and "South" along the edges of the board. Use the compass to make sure the edge marked "North" is facing toward the north.

Explanation: Winds are named after the direction *from which* the wind is blowing. When the arrow points toward the

▲ Some old-fashioned weather vanes have fanciful decorations and designs.

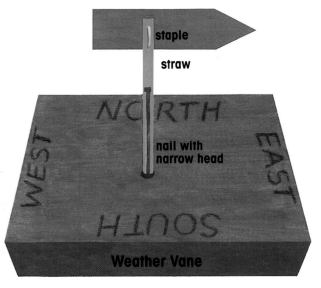

staple

straw

nail with narrow head

Weather Vane

west, it indicates a westerly wind—the wind is blowing from west to east. Your weather vane points into the wind because the pointed end of the cardboard (the smallest surface) receives the least amount of air pressure.

Rain Gauge

Materials needed: a coffee can and a ruler

Instructions: Place the coffee can outside. After it rains or snows, place the ruler in the can and measure the depth of the precipitation.

EXTRA EFFORT

If the precipitation in the can is snow, use your rain gauge to see how much water the snow contains. After measuring the depth of the snow, take your rain gauge indoors, let the snow melt, and measure the depth of the water. How much water comes from an inch of snow?

◀ Most rain gauges are simple. They measure the height of rainwater collecting in a tube.

Weather Shelter

Materials needed: a stand (a picnic table or a large garbage can turned upside down will work well) and a large wooden or cardboard box.

Instructions: Position the stand outdoors, in a shady area if possible, and keep it at least 3 feet from any buildings. Make sure there are plenty of holes in the sides of the box so that it won't get too hot inside. Turn the box upside down and place it on top of the stand. Put your thermometer and hygrometer inside the box and your anemometer, weather vane, and rain gauge on top of the box. Keep your barometer in the box or inside the house.

Explanation: The thermometer and hygrometer are placed inside the box because they should always be kept dry. The box should be kept a few feet above the ground and away from buildings so that heat from the ground or buildings doesn't damage the measurements. (Unlike store-bought weather instruments, your instruments might not hold up in rough weather. Occasionally, you might have to repair your instruments or build new ones.)

You're now ready to make your own weather observations. Try to record your measurements at about the same time each day. If possible, take your measurements more than once a day. Make a chart on a large sheet of paper or poster board with columns labeled "Day," "Time," "Air Pressure," "Temperature," "Relative Humidity," "Wind Speed," "Wind Direction," "Precipitation," "Clouds," and "Comments."

As you record patterns in the weather, you can begin to

What the professionals use: weather shelters, holding a variety of weather instruments, are located at weather stations throughout the United States. Scientists check the instruments regularly and send measurements to the National Weather Service.

make your own forecasts. Suppose your log shows southeasterly winds and cirrus clouds in the morning. A few hours later you see altostratus clouds, and the next entry shows nimbostratus clouds. You've spotted an approaching warm front. Keep taking measurements and see if your forecast is correct. Do the temperature and relative humidity increase? Does the wind change direction?

Compare your weather predictions with those reported on television, radio, or in the newspaper. With practice and experience, your forecasts should become more and more accurate. You'll learn to appreciate the beauty, power, and complexity of the weather, and you'll also have a lot of fun. Maybe you'll decide to become a professional meteorologist someday.

GLOSSARY

air mass: a large body of air with roughly the same temperature and relative humidity throughout the whole mass

air pressure: the force of air pressing against the Earth's surface

anemometer: an instrument used to measure wind speed

atmosphere: the blanket of air surrounding the Earth

barometer: an instrument used to measure air pressure

climate: the typical weather of a region

cold front: the boundary created when a cold air mass bumps into a warm air mass

condensation: the process in which water vapor changes into liquid water. Falling temperatures cause condensation.

Doppler radar: a radar system that compares the frequency of outgoing and incoming radio waves. Doppler radar is used to determine wind speed and direction.

evaporation: the process in which liquid water changes into water vapor. Evaporation is caused by heat.

forecast: as used in meteorology, a prediction about the weather

front: the boundary between a warm air mass and a cold air mass

high pressure system: a large area, circled by winds, with high pressure in the center of the system and low pressure around the outside

hygrometer: an instrument used to measure relative humidity

low pressure system: a large area, circled by winds, with low pressure in the center of the system and high pressure around the outside

meteorology: the science that involves measuring, studying, and predicting the weather

occluded front: the boundary created when a cold front overtakes a warm front

precipitation: liquid or frozen water that falls from the sky (usually rain or snow)

pressure systems: large areas under either high or low pressure, circled by winds

prevailing winds: giant wind belts that circle the Earth

radar: as used in weather forecasting, a system of radio signals that bounce off raindrops and snowflakes in clouds. Scientists analyze returning signals to locate clouds and storms.

radiosonde: a group of weather instruments attached to a hydrogen-filled balloon. Radiosondes are used to measure conditions high in the atmosphere.

rain gauge: an instrument—usually a tube or a bucket—used to measure rainfall

relative humidity: the amount of water vapor in the air

satellite: as used in weather forecasting, a spacecraft that orbits the Earth and takes photographs and readings of atmospheric conditions

stationary front: the boundary between two air masses that are moving alongside one another

thermometer: a device used to measure temperature

warm front: the boundary created when a warm air mass bumps into a cold air mass

water vapor: water in gas form

weather vane: an instrument that turns with the wind to indicate wind direction

INDEX

The Punxsutawney (Pennsylvania) Groundhog Club thinks spring.

METRIC CONVERSION CHART		
When you know:	**multiply by:**	**to find:**
acres	.41	hectares
square miles	2.59	square kilometers
gallons	3.79	liters
inches	2.54	centimeters
feet	.30	meters
yards	.91	meters
miles	1.61	kilometers
pounds	.45	kilograms
tons	.91	metric tons
degrees Fahrenheit	.56 (after subtracting 32)	degrees Celsius

ACKNOWLEDGMENTS

Photographs and illustrations used with permission of National Weather Service/National Oceanic and Atmospheric Administration: p. 2; Harry M. Walker Photography: pp. 7, 22, 28, 50, 55, 64 (left); The Bettmann Archive: p. 9; Sonny Eliot: p. 10; National Center for Atmospheric Research/National Science Foundation: pp. 11, 46, 49, 53; Betty Sederquist: p. 13; Frank S. Balthis: pp. 14, 41; Erwin C. "Bud" Nielson, Tucson, Ariz.: pp. 17 (top), 45; Betty Crowell: p. 17 (bottom); Steve Warble: p. 18 (both); Eda Rogers: pp. 20, 60, 62, 65; David Molchos: pp. 21, 39; Winston Fraser: pp. 25, 67; Liz Monson: pp. 27, 31 (both), 36 (both), 57 (left), 59 (left), 61, 63, 64 (right); National Aeronautics and Space Administration: p. 32; Star Tribune/WeatherData, Inc.: p. 43; Star Tribune/WeatherData, Inc./John Erste: p. 47; Tom Pantages: p. 57 (right); Nancy Smedstad: p.59 (right); The Punxsutawney Spirit: p. 71.

Front cover: Nancy Smedstad. Used with permission of KARE-TV, Minneapolis, Minn.